Layout and Drawings
by Laurie C

Cover Background Design by
Merlin Lightpainter, offered by Pexels.com

GROWN-UP JOKES

a collection of
colorful "off-color" jokes

Kittrick DaPont

p. 58 picture of Scottish man with kilt: photo by Hywel Williams, from Portfolio, UK

ISBN: 9798851479656

I'd like to dedicate this book to
my Dear Old Dad
who loved jokes so much that he's
probably still laughing in his grave.

Minds are like parachutes.
They only work when they're open.

About Kittrick DaPont

As a child around the age of eight, Kittrick heard his first jokes—his jovial, jokester father being the teller. Ever after, he had a fascination for jokes and the gift of memory that makes a good joke collector into a good joke teller.

Nowadays, he collects jokes at the local flea markets around Santa Cruz, California, from the cable guy, from vendors, from clients—from just about anyone anywhere. He begins the conversation with a joke of his own and then people often step up and share a "good one."

∞∞

Kittrick does a daily meditation upon awakening followed by a thirty-minute workout. His interests include organic gardening, bird-watching, hiking, and fishing. He is a long-time friend of Bill W.

SUBJECTS

Marriage

Kittrick's favorite joke at age eight:

A woman is married to a man who has everything. It's his birthday, and she's browsing for an unusual present. She goes to a pet store and asks for a special pet. The owner takes her to the back room where she sees a critter covered with long hair and huge teeth.

"*What is that?*" she asks.

"*It's a dingbat.*"

"*What does it do?*"

He shows her, saying: "*Dingbat chair!*"

The dingbat pounces, and shreds the chair.

"*Perfect!*" she says.

She buys it, and places the cage in a corner of the living room. Her husband comes home from work in a foul mood.

"*What in hell is that?*" he asks.

"*That's dingbat, Dear.*"

"*Dingbat my ass!!*"

A middle-age couple go to a marriage counselor, and at the end of the session the counselor grabs the wife, picks her up out of her chair, and begins passionately hugging and kissing her. She becomes highly aroused. The counselor looks at her husband and says,

"See that? That is what your wife needs at least once a day."

The husband replies,

"Well, let's see. I can bring her on Mondays and Tuesdays, but on Wednesdays I golf."

∞

A man comes home from work unexpectedly. He hears commotion coming from the upstairs bedroom. He goes up there, peeks in the bedroom, and finds his wife and his best friend in bed together. He storms in and yells,

"What in the hell is going on here?"

His wife turns to her lover and says,

"See? I told you he was stupid."

A young newlywed couple go to a church to see about becoming members. The priest says,

"The only condition is that you have to be celibate for three weeks before you can join."

The first week goes smoothly. The second week they begin to look at one another lustfully. Five days into the third week, the wife bends over to pick up a watermelon and her husband is overcome with desire, so they get it on right then and there.

They return to the church and plead with the priest.

"We were only two days shy of making it to three weeks."

The priest answers,

"Sorry. You're no longer welcome in our church."

The couple reply,

"Yeah, we understand. We're no longer welcome at Safeway either."

∞

A gal was talking to her spouse:

"Have you heard that Harry in apartment 25 died last night after just eight weeks of marriage?"

Her husband replied,

"Well, at least his suffering was cut short."

The groom and best man are walking up the aisle to the altar, and the best man says,

"You're so calm and colletced. I was very nervous on my wedding day."

The groom says,

"I'm marrying the most wonderful woman on the planet, and she just gave me the most incredible blow job! I'm looking forward to having that for the rest of my life."

The bride and bridesmaid are walking behind the groom, and the bridesmaid says,

"Why the huge smile on your face?"

The bride says,

" I just gave my last blow job!

A gal goes to the pharmacist and says,

"I need some cyanide for my husband, please."

The pharmacist says,

"I can't do that. Not only is it highly illegal, but I could lose my license."

The lady pulls out a photo of her husband getting it on with the pharmacist's wife. He looks at the photograph and says, "How much do you need?"

A doctor is going on a business trip, but his young wife who is staying at home needs constant sexual attention. He goes to an adult novelty store and brings her a voodoo dildo that operates on voice command. He explains to her:

"When you want it to perform, you say, 'Voodoo dildo my vagina.' When you are sated, say 'Voodoo dildo stop.'"

So after the husband leaves, she tries it out. When she's sated, she says: "Voodoo dildo stop." But it won't stop, so she gets in the car and heads to the hospital to have it removed.

She's driving erratically and gets pulled over. She explains to the officer about the voodoo dildo and why she's driving so haphazardly. The officer replies,

"Voodoo dildo my ass!"

∞

A guy comes home from work, and his wife is lying on their bed breathing rapidly.

"I think I'm having a heart attack, Honey!" she utters breathlessly.

Meanwhile, their young daughter rushes in crying,

"Daddy, Daddy! There's a naked man in the closet!"

He looks, and it's his best friend Herb, standing there. He yells,

"Ethel's having a heart attack, and you're running around naked, scaring the kids?"

An 86-year-old man proposes to an 18-year-old. She says: "Before I accept your proposal I need to know three things: *First: I need my own bathroom.*"

He answers, *"There are four bathrooms in the main house. Take your pick."*

"Second: I want a place on the beach."

He answers, *"I have a place right on the sand in St. Petes. What's your third question?"*

She says, *"What about sex?"*

He answers, *"Infrequently."*
She asks, *"Is that one word or two?"*

∞

A couple go to a marriage counselor and say,
   "Our love life is getting boring, jaded. What can you suggest to spice it up?"
The counselor recommends,

   "Well, you have to experiment with different positions, not the same old missionary one. For instance, try the 'wheelbarrow.' Both of you get undressed. Your wife lies on the floor, and you grab her by her ankles and enter her as she starts walking on her hands."

Driving back home he says,
   "I'm getting really excited thinking about doing the 'wheelbarrow.'"
She says, *"I'll do it on two conditions: One: If I don't like it we have to stop immediately. Two: We can't go past my parents' house."*

A priest gets upset about all his parishioners coming to confession with their sins of adultery. He gets on his pulpit and announces:

"All you confessing to adultery, I've had it! If it continues, I'm closing down the church!"

His parishioners like him and the church, and don't want him to close, so they get together and make up a code word for adultery; the word is "fallen." Years pass, and the priest retires, and a new priest takes his place. In his first sermon, he addresses the mayor who is in the congregation:

"Mr. Mayor, you have to fix your sidewalks. People complain every day about falling."

The mayor laughs because he knows the code word. The priest says,

"I don't know what you're laughing about. Your own wife fell three times last week!"

∞

A married couple is eating dinner in a restaurant. There's a man sitting at the next table, obviously really drunk, and he's eyeing the wife. Her husband says,

"Do you know that man?"

She says: *"He was my husband ten years ago, and he's been drunk like that ever since."*

Her husband says,

"I didn't think anyone could celebrate that long!"

A couple, searching the world over for true love, find each other. They plan a lavish wedding with friends and family. The only problem is that his fiancée's younger sister is always wearing short skirts and saying suggestive things.

One afternoon, the sister invites him over to help make out wedding invitations. She's wearing the shortest skirt yet, and begins walking up the stairs to the bedroom, shedding clothing as she goes. She gets to the landing, takes off her panties, and they sail down the staircase and hit him in the face. He bolts for the front door. He opens the door, and his fiancée and father-in-law are standing there with tears in their eyes. The father- in-law gives him a bear hug and says,

"Son, I'm so proud of you. You passed our little test."

Moral: Always keep your condoms in your glove compartment.

A couple is watching a Discovery Channel episode about an African tribe. In that culture, when boys reach puberty they have a big weight hung on their penis. When they reach manhood, they're more than *eighteen* inches long.

His wife says,

"You know, you ought to try that. You could use a few extra inches."

A week later she asks,

"How's our little experiment going, Honey?"

He says, *"I'm half-way there."*

She asks, *"You mean you're sporting nine inches?"*

He answers,

"No, it's turned all black, though."

∞

Dr. Bob and his wife are on the beach sitting on chaise lounges admiring the surf, when a hot young thing jogs by wearing a string bikini. She sees them and says,

"Good morning, Dr. Bob," and continues on her jog.

Bob's wife says, *"Where do you know her from?"*

The doctor answers, *"Oh, she's just someone I met professionally."*

Bob's wife asks, *"Whose profession, yours or hers?"*

What is a honeymoon salad?   Lettuce alone.
No dressing.

∞

Two neighbors meet at the mailbox and one says,
"You need to get some curtains in your bedroom win-
dow. Our living room looks right down on your bed-
room, and you were putting on quite a show for my wife
and me last night."

The other man says,
"You must be mistaken. I wasn't even home last night."

∞

After twenty-eight years of married life, Harry was
scrutinizing his wife, and muttered,

"Twenty-eight years ago we had a shabby flat, a clunker
of a car, and we slept on a hide-a-bed. The nice thing
was, I slept with a twenty-two-year-old knockout. To-
day, we live in a fancy home with a new car and sleep
in a luxurious bed. Unfortunately, I'm sharing it with a
forty-eight-year-old gal. If you ask me, I'm getting the
short end of the stick."

She said,
"If you're so nostalgic, go ahead and find yourself a
twenty-two-year-old bombshell, and I will guarantee
you'll wind up in a shabby flat with a clunker of a car,
and you'll be sleeping in a hide-a-bed."

What does the Polish woman get on her wedding night that's long and hard?

A new last name.

∞

It's the mailman's last day on the job. He rings the doorbell. The housewife shows up in a sheer negligée and says,

"Come on in. I've got breakfast for you."

He sits down to a wonderful breakfast and coffee. Then they head to the upstairs bedroom. They get it on, and she slips him a dollar.

He asks, *"What's this all about?"*

She responds,

"I told my husband last night that it was your last day, and I wanted to do something special for you. He said, 'Fuck him! Give him a dollar.' Breakfast was my idea."

This stockbroker comes home and tells his wife that the market took a huge dip, and their income took a dive. He says,

"If you learned how to cook and clean a little, we could fire the maid."

Her reply:

"If you learned how to fuck, we could fire the gardener."

∞

Two guys are playing golf, and there are two women in front of them playing slowly. One man says,

"I'll go and see if they'll let us play through."

He gets closer and realizes it's his wife and his mistress, so he goes back to his buddy and tells him what happened.

His buddy says, *"Let me try."*

He comes back with a sheepish look on his face and says,

"Small world isn't it?"

Richard Nixon and Sammy Davis Jr. are attending a charity ball. They both wind up standing next to each other at the urinal in the men's room. Richard glances down and says,

"Geez Sammy, you sure are well hung."
Sammy says, *"I wasn't born this way. Every night before I go to bed, I grab it and whack it against the bedpost."*

Richard says, *"Really!"* and

Sammy says, *"No shit."*

Richard gets home late, and Pat is already asleep in bed. He gets undressed and whacks it against the bedpost. Pat jumps up and yells,

"Sammy, is that you?"

∞

A couple is dining in an upscale restaurant. In the middle of dinner, the man starts sliding down his chair and ends up under the table with the tablecloth obscuring him. The waitress comes to the table and whispers to the lady,

"Your husband just slid under the table."
She says,

"No he didn't. He just walked in the front door."

A husband is walked all over by his wife. He finally decides to get assertiveness training. He goes to a session, comes back, and starts ordering her around. He asserts,

"I'm going out tonight. Guess who's going to dress me, shave me, and part my hair?"

She answers, *"The undertaker."*

∞

These two newlyweds are finally done with their reception. She is waiting in their bed, looking forward to a night of passion. He is very pious, and she finds him down on floor praying by the bed.

She asks, *"What are you doing?"*
He responds, *"I'm praying for salvation."*

She says, *"Get up here. I'll pray for salvation. You pray for endurance."*

This gal is talking with her gynecologist and she says,

"I have a problem you might be able to help me with. I'm engaged, and my fiancé thinks I'm a virgin, but I'm not."

Her gynecologist responds,

"There's nothing medically I can do, but I understand that some gals in your situation get a thick rubber band and work it onto their upper thigh. When hubby enters her, she gives it a good snap and tells him it's her hymen snapping."

She says,

"He's not that bright. That will probably work. Thanks for the info."

They have a lavish wedding and wind up in their honeymoon suite. She goes into the bathroom to get dolled up and slips a rubber band onto her upper thigh. They both hop into bed. He enters her, and she snaps the rubber band. He exclaims in a shaky voice, *"W...What the hell is that???"*

She answers, *"That was my hymen snapping, Sweetheart."*

He says, in a trembling voice, *"Can you unsnap it? It's wrapped all around my balls."*

∞

How do you know when a guy's a loser?
When he's gettin' it on, he fantasizes he's somebody else.

This fireman is talking with his wife. He explains,

"Down at the firehouse we have this procedure. In case of emergency, we have one bell that goes off. If it's really important, two bells go off. If it's a dire emergency, three bells. I'd like to incorporate that into our love life. For the first bell, we'll meet up in the bedroom and start foreplay. The second bell, we're going to get undressed and start heavy petting. The third bell, we make love."

So the first bell goes off, and they run upstairs to the bedroom and start their foreplay. The second bell rings, and they undress and begin heavy petting. At the third bell, they are making love.

She shouts, *"Now, bell number four!"*

He inquires, *"What's bell number four?"*

She elaborates, *"Roll out more hose. You're nowhere near the fire."*

∞

Matrimony is difficult. In the first year, the guy does all the talking, and the woman listens.

In the second year, the woman does all the talking, and the guy listens.

In the third year, they're both talking, and the neighborhood listens.

A flasher flashed three old ladies sitting on a park bench. The first one had a stroke. The second one had a stroke.

The third lady's arms weren't long enough to reach.

∞

A businessman has been away on three-day trip. He takes a cab home from the airport and confides in the cabbie,

"I think there's some funny business going on with the wife. Can you accompany me home?"

They get there and, sure enough, she's in bed with another man. He rips the blanket off and holds a pistol to the man's head.

His wife says,

"Just a minute. Remember when your business was going belly-up, and I came into thousands of dollars and helped it from going under? That was thanks to this man. You know that membership we have in the exclusive country club? That's also thanks to this man. And the nice, new Mercedes in the garage? You can thank this man."

So he turns to the cabbie and says, *"What should I do?"*

The cabbie answers,

"He looks cold. You'd better cover him back up."

A guy woke up Saturday morning with a horrific hangover. He called to his wife and asked,

"What happened last night?"
She responded,
"You made a complete ass of yourself. Your boss was at the podium giving an inspirational talk to his employees, and you got up there and told him he was a dumb jerk."

He asked, *"Then what happened?"*

She said, *"Well, he fired you."*

He replied, *"Well, fuck him!"*

She said, *"I did. You go back to work Monday."*

∞

This guy is really down in the dumps. His best friend is trying to cheer him up and says,
"Whats going on, buddy?"
The guy replies,
"My wife came home this morning and I asked her where she'd been last night and she said: 'I spent the night at my sister's.'

She couldn't have, because I spent the night at her sister's."

What did Melinda Gates say after her honeymoon with Bill?

"Now I see why you named it Microsoft."

∞

A newlywed couple is getting ready to make love, and before he can mount her, a bee flies into her vagina. They call the doctor, and he says to get her over there as quickly as possible.

The doctor says,

"I'm going to put some honey on my penis and see if I can lure him out with that."

The husband comes into the room and sees the doctor furiously pumping away.

The husband asks, *"What's going on here?"*

The doctor pants,

"Change of plans. I'm going to drown the little bastard."

∞

This gal is in bed for hours with her husband's best friend, and the phone rings. Her hubby's best friend hears her side of the conversation. In a nonchalant tone, she says,

"I hope you're having a wonderful time."

She hangs up, and the best friend says, *"Who was that?"*

She replies, *"That was my husband. He's having a great time fishing with you."*

An artist is working at home, and his model comes in to pose for a painting. He says,

"I know we agreed on this time, but I feel really rotten. I think I'm coming down with something. I'll pay you for showing up, but I'm just going to have some tea and go to bed."

She says, *"Well let me fix it for you."*

He adds, *"Fix yourself some while you're at it."*

They're sitting drinking tea when he hears the door open, and he hears his wife say, *"Honey I'm home."*

He turns to the model and says,
"It's my wife! Quick take off all your clothes."

∞

Four ways that "fucking," for a man, changes over the marriage years:

One: In the beginning you and she have sex all over the house: on the floor in the living room, on the kitchen table, in the hallway—every room in the house.

Two: Years later, it's mainly in the bedroom.

Three: More years go by, and you say, *"Fuck you!"* when you meet up in the hall.

Four: When she and her divorce attorney fuck you for every penny you have in a courtroom full of onlookers.

After years of frustration, the Turners still have no children, so they decided to use a proxy to start their family. On the day he was to arrive, her husband kisses her and says, *"The man should be here shortly."*

Forty-five minutes goes by, and a baby photographer knocks on the door. He says,

"Good afternoon, ma'am. I'm Mr. Schott. I've come to. . ."

Mrs. Turner interrupts: *"No need to explain. I've been expecting you."*

Mr. Schott exclaims, *"Great! Babies are my specialty."*

Mrs. Turner says, *"Come on in. Where do we start?"*

Mr. Schott replies, *"I normally do three in the tub, two on the floor, and perhaps a couple in bed."*

Mrs. Turner shouts, *"Tub? Floor? I can see why it didn't work for my husband and me."*

Mr. Schott adds, *"I usually shoot from **sixty-five** different angles to make sure there's a good one."*

Mrs. Turner says, *"Hopefully this won't take too long."*

Mr. Schott explains, *"In my profession, I need to take my time. I could be in and out in three or four minutes, but I'm sure you'd be unhappy."*

Mrs. Turner states, *"You're damned right!"*

The photographer opens his briefcase and pulls out an album of babies. He says,

"These twins were the result of my efforts, even though the mother struggled and was uncooperative."

Mrs. Turner asks, *"She was uncooperative?"*

Mr. Schott replies, *"She sure was. We wound up going to Hyde Park to get it done. A huge crowd of onlookers gathered to watch."*

Mrs. Turner, incredulous, exclaims, *"A huge crowd?"*

Mr. Schott replies, *"The mother was out of control, screaming, creating a huge scene, and it was hard for me to get the job done. It began to get dark, and I had to force my last shots in a hurry. It's getting late. We should get started. Let me unfold my tripod so we can begin."*

Mrs. Turner (distraught) questions, *"Tripod? What's that for?"*

Mr. Schott explains, *"I need it to steady my Canon. It's huge and heavy, and I can't hold it still while I'm on the verge of action."*

"Ma'am? Ma'am?
Good God, she's fainted."

∞

Two gay Irishmen: Patrick Fitzgerald and
Gerald Fitzpatrick

A man is sick and tired of his wife. He tells his buddy that he can't stand her anymore and wants to hire a hitman.

His buddy suggests,

"I've got just the guy for you, Big Artie. He hangs out in this local bar and likes his work so much he'll do it for a dollar."

The man goes to the bar and hires Big Artie. Big Artie shadows his wife for days and finally follows her to a deserted shopping mall. He sneaks up behind her and strangles her. As he's lowering her lifeless body to the courtyard, he looks up and sees two old ladies who had just come around the corner. He runs over and strangles both of them.

The headlines in the papers the next day read:

"Artichokes Three for a Dollar"

∞

Mickey and Minnie Mouse are in divorce court.

The judge asks Mickey,

"Are you asking for a divorce on the grounds that your wife, Minnie Mouse, is crazy?"

Mickey answers, *"I didn't say that, Your Honor. I said, 'She's fuckin' Goofy.'"*

This gal in New York City leaves her apartment and goes to her corner grocery store. She buys a case of cat food.

The owner wonders,
> "Why are you buying cat food? You don't even own a cat."

She says,
> "It's for my husband. He loves it."

The owner says,
> "It's no good for him. You'd better stop, or he'll get sick and die."

A week later, the owner is reading the obituaries and sees that the wife's husband has passed away. The next time she comes in, he says,

> "I'm sorry for your loss, but I warned you this would happen if you fed him cat food."

She says,
> "Nonsense. He was lying in the street licking his ass and got run over by a truck."

∞

What's the difference between an Irish wake and an Irish wedding?

One less drunken Irishman.

Families and
Smart Kids

A young couple take their six-year-old son to the nude beach. Mom lays out their beach blanket. The son walks up the beach, returns, and says,

"Mommy, I saw some women who have breasts bigger than yours."

Mom says,

"The bigger they are, the dumber they are."

The son walks up the beach again.

"Mommy, I saw some men that have peepees bigger than Daddy's."

Mom answers,

"The bigger they are the dumber they are."

This time he walks down the beach instead of up the beach, and returns with a worried look on his face. The son exclaims,

"Mommy, Daddy's talking to the dumbest girl on the beach, and the longer he talks the dumber he gets."

∞

A three-year-old and his five-year-old brother are watching TV with their family. The mother catches the father's eye, and they head upstairs. The five-year-old goes upstairs to use the bathroom and notices the bedroom door is cracked open. He gets on his knees, takes a peek, and goes back downstairs to the TV. He gestures to his brother:

"Come here. You have to see this."

The three-year-old kneels down and peeks, and his eyes get as big as saucers. The five-year-old says,

"And to think she's the same lady who paddled our asses for sucking our thumbs."

A ten-year-old approaches his girlfriend's father and says,

"Me and Sally are in love, and I'm asking for her hand in marriage."

The father thinks this is cutest thing he's ever heard and says,

"How are you going to support her, and where will you live?"

The boy says,

"I get ten dollars a week for my allowance, and Sally gets fifteen, and her bedroom's bigger than mine, so we're moving in there."

The father thinks, *Wow! They've really thought this out.* He says, "Well, what's going to happen when the little ones arrive?"

The kid says, *"So far we've been really lucky."*

Dad walks into his son's room unexpectedly and catches him masturbating.

He says, *"You know if you keep doing that you'll go blind."*

The son says, *"Dad, I'm over here!"*

∞

A family goes to the circus, and Dad goes to get popcorn. The six-year-old son tugs on his mother's arm and asks,

"What's that hanging under the elephant?"

Mom answers, *"That's the elephant's tail, Son."*

He says, *"I know what the tail looks like. What's that other thing?"*

Mom looks and blushes: *"Oh, that? That's nothing."*

Dad comes back. His son tugs on his arm and asks,

"Daddy, what's that hanging under the elephant?"

"That's his tail, son."

"I know, but what's that other thing?"

"That's the elephant's penis, Son."

"How come when I asked Mommy what it was, she said it's nothing?"

Dad says, "I've spoiled that woman, Son."

A five-year-old is talking to his three-year-old brother:
"I heard some of the big kids talking the other day. They don't talk anything like us. They say all kinds of cool things like: 'What the hell?' and 'You bet your sweet ass!' I'm going to start acting more grown-up and talking like them."

The three-year old says, *"Me too!"*

The next morning at breakfast, their father says to the five-year-old,
"What are you going to have for breakfast, Son?"
His son replies,
"What the hell, Dad. I think I'll have cocoa puffs."

The father reaches across the table and slaps him, and then he asks the three-year-old,
*"What are **you** going to have, Son?"*

The three-year-old stutters,
"I..I don't know. But you can bet your sweet ass it won't be cocoa puffs!"

∞

"Once I went twelve years without any sex, drugs, or alcohol. My dad sure knew how to throw a birthday party for a thirteen-year-old."

When I was a wee lad, my folks would take me out in the rowboat. When we got about a mile out, they'd drop me overboard. I kind of enjoyed the swim back, but it was a bitch getting out of that sack.

∞

The little granddaughter says,   *"Grandma, Grandma, can you make a noise like a frog?"*

Grandma says,   *"Sure I can, Honey, but why?"*

The granddaughter says,
   "I overheard Daddy talking to Mommy, and he says we're going to be filthy rich as soon as you croak."

∞

While body surfing, this gal loses her top. As she's stepping onto the crowded beach, she crosses her arms over her chest. She's rushing to get back to her towel, when a little eight-year-old boy blocks her path and says,

   "If you're giving those puppies away, Miss, I'll take the one with the pink nose."

Mr. Rabbit is waiting for his son to come home after school. He arrives home, bouncing off the walls, with a huge grin on his face. Mr. Rabbit asks,
"*Why are you so happy, Son?*"
His son says, "*Today we had the math quiz.*"

Mr. Rabbit inquires, "*So?*"

His son responds, "*They taught us how to multiply.*"

∞

A girl goes to her daddy and tells him:
"*John proposed to me last night.*"

Her dad says, "*Oh that's wonderful, Sweetheart!*"

She says,
"*No it's not! It'll never work. He doesn't believe there's a God, and he doesn't believe there's a hell.*"

The father responds,
"*Don't worry, Sweetheart. Between you and your mother, you'll show him there's a hell.*"

∞

I've always wondered how I'd know if I was truly in love. I'd ask myself,
Would I mind if this person took me for everything I've got?

An old man's son has finally persuaded him to go to a rest home, and he reluctantly goes. The first morning, he wakes up with an erection, and a pretty young nurse comes in, notices it, and gives him an incredible blow-job. Afterward, he gets on the phone with his son:

"You know I had my doubts about this place, but I think I'm going to love it here."

He's in the corridor after lunch with his walker. He falls down, and an orderly comes and rips his pants off, has his way with him, and leaves him there in the corridor. The old man calls his son again and says,

"You have to get me out of here right now!"

The son says, *"I thought you loved it there."*

The father responds,

"The problem is, I get a hard on two or three times a year, but I fall down a couple times a day."

∞

Mom and Dad approach their thirteen-year-old son and say, *"What do you want for your birthday?"*

The son replies, *"I wanna watch."*

And so they let him.

A teacher is talking to her fifth-graders and says,
"What do you want to be when you grow up, Larry?"

Larry says,
"I want to be an inventor and invent something that half the world's population can't do without. I'm going to have a villa in Spain and a chalet in France and I'm going down to Monte Carlo and find me a fine little whore and spoil her rotten, and she's going to have a Ferrari and a private jet to go anywhere she wants, and every night I'm gonna' be banging her like a loose screen door in a hurricane."

The teacher shouts,
*"Stop! That's enough! What do **you** want to be, Sally?"*

Sally replies, *"I want to be Larry's little whore."*

∞

A teenage boy slipped into a strip tease venue, and somehow his mother found out about it.

His mother questioned him,
"You didn't see anything you shouldn't have, did you?"

The boy replied, *"Yup, I did. I saw Dad."*

A man is making love with his wife, and his three-year-old son comes into the bedroom and says,

"*Horsey ride! Horsey ride!*"

So the dad says, "*What the hell,*" and lets him ride on his back.

Mom's eyes glaze over, and the son says,

"*Hang on, Dad. This is when me and the mailman get bucked off.*"

∞

Which is tastier: an earth rock or a space rock?
A space rock. It's a little "meteor."

∞

A father walks with his five-year-old son in the park. His son pulls his dad's sleeve and points:

"*Daddy, Daddy, what are those two dogs doing?*"

Dad explains,

"*Well, it appears to me the one dog has hurt his paws. The other dog is helping him cross the hot asphalt.*"

The son takes another look and says,

"*Isn't that just the way it is, Dad! Try and help your friend, and you get fucked every time.*"

There are teenage twins, a guy and gal. The sister says, *"If you haven't got a date to the prom yet, I would like to go with you."*

He retorts, *"You're my sister. That's disgusting!"*

It turns out he doesn't have a date, so he ends up taking his sister. They're standing around watching everyone dance, and the sister says, *"Let's dance."*

He snorts, *"You're my sister. That's gross."*

Rather than standing around, they start dancing. After the prom, he's driving them home, and she says,

"Let's stop off at Lovers Lane."

He says incredulously, *"You're my sister. That's disgusting!"*

She says, *"We haven't had a talk for awhile. I just want to sit there and talk."*

They park at Lovers Lane, and she jumps in the back seat and says, *"Come back here."*

He goes back and mounts her, and she says,

"You know something? You're a lot lighter than Dad."

And he says, *"That's what Mom says too."*

∞

Why do women have such a hard time finding men who are sensitive, handsome, and charming?

Those men already have boyfriends.

A rancher woman is entertaining her friends at a luncheon in her home. Her ten-year-old son, Johnny, comes bursting in and says,
  "Mommy, Mommy! The bull is shagging the cow."

His mother, embarrassed, says to him,
  *"You can't talk like that, especially in front of my girlfriends. In the future, say: The bull is **surprising** the cow."*

Johnny leaves, and ten minutes later he runs back in all excited. He yells,
  *"Mommy, Mommy! The bull is surprising **all** the cows!"*

Mommy says, "That's impossible!"

Johnny replies, *"No it's not. He's shagging the horse."*

∞

Two teachers were chaperoning their third-grade students to the horse races. They took the boys to the men's room and the urinals were too high, so they unzipped the boys and boosted them up so they could pee.

One teacher glanced down and saw that her student was really well endowed. She said,
  "What grade are you in?"
The student replied,
  "I'll be riding Silver Streak in the fourth."

A mother gets an urgent phone call from school. Evidently her ten-year-old son locked himself and a little girl in the cafeteria, and it took forty-five minutes to get them out. The mother later interrogated him about what happened in the forty-five minutes.

The son declared, *"Well I showed her my thing."*

Mom asked, *"And then what happened?"*

The son replied, *"She showed me **her** thing."*

Mom inquired, *"And then what happened?"*

The son said, *"Well, one thing led to another."*

∞

True Story:

My uncle had just passed. My cousins were there from LA for the memorial. The neighbor, a good Christian who had known them since they were children, saw them in the driveway and stopped to give them his condolences.

My auntie, who was suffering from dementia, opened the front door, saw him out there, and hollered out,

"What's that cocksucker doing here?"

Men

Two young guys go into a general store. There's a big bread rack on the back wall going all the way to the ceiling. Noting that all the raisin bread is on the top rack **and** noticing the clerk's mini-skirt, the first young man orders a raisin bread. After she climbs back down, the second guy says,

"Miss, I need a loaf of raisin bread too!"

So she climbs up and down again, the guys getting a good view. Two more guys walk in. They quickly catch on and order raisin bread too. While she's still up there getting the fourth loaf, an old man walks in. Trying to avoid another trip up and down the ladder, she yells from up there,

"Is yours raisin too?"

He responds,

"No, not quite, but it is twitchin' a mite."

A cowboy is riding on the range . He comes across an Indian lying on his back with a huge erection.

The cowboy asks,
"What are you doing?"

The Indian replies, *"My penis sundial. Me tell time. It now 2:00."*

The cowboy looks at his watch and sees that it actually is 2:00. He rides on and comes to another Indian lying there with an erection. He also says his penis is a sundial and that it reads 3:00. The cowboy rides on and comes to one at 4:00, 5:00, and so forth.

Finally, he comes to an Indian who is lying there masturbating.
"What are you doing?" he asks.
"Me wind watch." answers the Indian.

∞

A pilot is on the intercom and announces,
"We'll be flying at 10,000 feet and the weather in LA is in the 70s. Thank you for flying with United."

He turns to the co-pilot and says,
"I'd sure ike to get into that new flight attendant's panties and have a cold beer."

The flight attendant hears this and rushes to the cockpit to tell him the intercom is still on. An old lady stops her and says,
"Wait a minute, Dearie. You've forgotten the cold beer."

There are two farmers living next door to one another. One day, the first farmer was looking for his neighbor and couldn't find him anywhere. He looked in the garden, the pasture, the big house, and he finally found him in the barn. His neighbor had his coveralls half off and was doing a slow, sexy strip tease in front of his John Deere. The first farmer says,

"It's really none of my business, but what in the hell are you doing?"

His neighbor answers,

"The missus and me are having marital problems. So we went to one of dem dar marriage counselors, and she suggested that I do something sexy to a tractor.

∞

True story:

My father and I went to the same urologist for years, and the instruction was always the same. Turn around, face the wall, bend over, and take your pants to half-mast. My father had assumed the position and turned to look back at the doctor.

The urologist said,

"What are you looking back here for?"

My father answered,

*"I'm just checking to make sure you still had **your** pants on!"*

A guy goes to his doctor. He was working on the roof, and he fell off and broke his leg. The doctor asks,

"How did this happen?"

The guy says,

"About twenty years ago, I got a job at a ranch. I was kick'n back in the bunk house after a hard day's work, and the rancher's daughter came in dressed in a low-cut blouse. She had baked me a pie. She brought it over, and I had a bite, and it was delicious. She leaned in close and said: 'Is there anything else I can do for you?'
I thought about it and said: 'No ma'am I can't think of anything.' She leaned in even closer and said, 'If you do think of anything, you'll let me know right away, won't you?'"

The doctor asks,

"That's an interesting story, but how does that pertain to breaking your leg?"

He replies,

"Well, this morning it dawned on me what she meant, and I fell off the roof."

This pirate walks into a bar. He has a patch over one eye, a pegleg, and a hook for his hand.

The bartender says, *"Man! What happened to you?"*
The pirate replies,
   "I was sailing the seven seas and this other pirate, Captain Blood 'n Guts, pulled up alongside and swung from his rigging onto my ship. He had a cutlass, and I drew mine, and he cut off my hand."

The bartender says, *"Sorry to hear that. What about your leg?"*

The pirate elaborates, *"I was sailing the seven seas and took a swim, and a shark came and bit my foot off."*

The bartender inquires, *"What about your eye?"*

The pirate continues, *"I was on deck sailing the seven seas, looked up, and a seagull flew over and shat right into my eye."*

The bartender asks, *"You lost your eye over that?"*

The pirate replies, *"Nope, it was my first day with the hook."*

∞

The captain announces that the airplane is going down, about to crash. A young woman gets out in the aisle and rips off her blouse begging,
   "I want one of you men to make me feel like a woman."

A guy stands up, takes his shirt off, holds it out to her, and says, *"Iron this."*

A gringo goes down to Mexico to start a ranchero. He goes to the local marketplace and hollers to a vendor,

"How much for the donkey?"

"Oh no Señor," the vendor says. *"It's not a donkey. It's an ass."*

So he buys the ass and goes to the next vendor.

"Señor, how much for the rooster?" he asks.

The second vendor replies, *"Oh no, Señor, it's not a rooster. It's a cock."*

The gringo asks, *"How much for the hen?"*

"Señor, it's a pullet," the vendor replies.

So he buys the cock and the pullet and goes back to his ranchero on the outskirts of the village. The ass runs away, and there's this pretty señorita standing on the street corner.

The gringo implores,

"Señorita, Señorita, please can you grab my cock and pullet while I chase my ass?"

∞

An attractive young nurse is talking to the doctor in charge. She's trying to take the blood pressure of a young man in his late teens.

The nurse states, *"Everytime I take this man's blood pressure, it skyrockets. What should I do?"*

The doctor suggests, *"Blindfold him."*

A young Scottish lass went to a local pub and sat next to a Scottsman at the bar. The Scottsman was clad in a kilt. She said,

"I've always wondered what's worn under the kilt."

He said, *"Give me your hand, and I'll show you."*

He pulled her hand under the kilt, and she drew it back quickly and exclaimed, *"Gruesome!"*

He said, *"Check it out. It grew some more."*

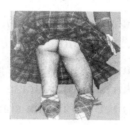

∞

Dan Quail had just graduated from the Airforce. He called his dad who said,

"Come over, Son, and tell me all about it."

Dan begin by saying:

"Yesterday was the parachute jump. Everyone jumped out of the plane but me. My commanding officer came up behind me and rested a hand on my shoulder. He said, 'Listen here, Son. I'm gay. You either jump out of this plane, or I'll have my way with you right here.'"

Dad inquired, *"Did you jump, Son?"*
Dan replied, *"A little, at first."*

above photo by Hywel Williams, from Portfolio, UK

A professor addresses her class and says,

"It's time to write a term paper. One third of your grade depends on it. It's due next Friday, and no excuses."

A wise guy in the back of the class pipes up,

"How about being physically, sexually exhausted?"

The professor says,

"Well in that case you'll have to use your other hand to write."

∞

God goes to the Garden of Eden and tells Adam,

"I've got some good news and some bad news."

Adam says,

"Tell me the good news first."

God continues,

"I've created you with two heads and you can think with either one of them."

Adam says,

"That's fantastic, God. Now tell me, what's the bad news?"

God replies,

"I've only given you enough blood to think with one of them at a time."

∞

What did the penis say to the condom?

"Cover me. I'm going in."

A sensitive young man saved all his money to vacation in Europe. He calls his brother back in the States and asks about his beloved cat.

The brother answers, *"I'm sorry. The cat died."*

He is grief-stricken and returns home immediately. He is very upset for weeks.

His brother says to him,
"I'm really sorry about the cat, but what could I have done?"

He replies,
"You could have broken the news to me more gently. For instance, you could have said, 'The cat's on the roof,' and then the next time I called, that the cat fell off the roof, and the next time, 'We did everything we could, but the cat passed away.'"

Years later, he's on vacation again. He calls his brother and asks, "How's mom doing?"

The brother replies, *"Mom's on the roof."*

∞

A man goes to his doctor and says,
"Doctor, I'm seeing pink crocodiles."

The doctor says,
"Have you seen a psychiatrist?"

The man replies,
"Nope. Just pink crocodiles."

An American businessman was invited to an Arabian sheik's compound to be entertained. That night the sheik lent him one of his wives, and while they were making love, she screamed out, *"Onga Bonga!"* very passionately.

The next morning, they were on the sheik's private golf course, and the sheik hit a hole in one.

The American yelled, *"Onga Bonga!"*

The sheik shouted, *"What do you mean, 'Wrong hole?'"*

∞

This guy stops dating altogether because he gets these enormous, unexpected erections that are really embarrassing. He finally gets over it and sets up an online date with a gal.

Just to be safe, he tapes his penis to his right leg. He rings the doorbell. She answers in a sheer negligée, and he kicks her in the face.

∞

How does a redneck pick up women?
He pulls up next to them and says,

   "Get in the truck."

∞

My mom nvever understood the irony of calling me a son of a bitch.

How to get rid of a case of the crabs:

First, you shave one side completely bald.

Then you light the other side on fire.

When they come crawling out of the fire, you stab them with an ice pick.

∞

A mid-thirties executive is tired of the bar scene. He decides he wants to settle down with a nice young gal and start a family. He takes the first girl out, wines and dines her.

She says, *"I had a great night. Let's fuck."*

Obviously, she's not the one. So he dates a succession of women with the same results. Finally, he dates this pretty young thing and she says,
   "I had a wonderful evening. We'll have to do it again some time."

He thinks: *Wow! She might be the one.*

A few dates later, they wind up in his apartment. They're getting undressed, and she says,
   "You have such a cute little wee wee."

He thinks: *Wow, she's young and innocent. She's the one.* So they have a lavish wedding. In the honeymoon suite they're getting undressed.

She says, *"You have such a cute little wee wee."*

He says, *"Now that we're married, I want you to know this isn't a wee wee. This is a cock."*

She says, *"No it isn't. Cocks are twelve inches long and they're black."*

A mid-thirties executive is talking with his psychiatrist.

He says,

"Doctor, you have to help me. I get up in the morning and do the wife. I catch a carpool to work and get a blow job from one of the gals in the carpool. I get to work and take my receptionist into the stock room. I take my secretary to lunch and do her. I get home and the housekeeper is still there, so I do her. By then, my wife's home from work so I do her again."

The doctor exclaims, *"Son, you've got to get a hold of yourself."*

He replies,

"I do that too, several times a day. It doesn't seem to help."

∞

What is Clinton soup?

A weeny in hot water.

∞

Why is sperm white, and pee is yellow?

To let you know if you're coming or going.

Women

A gringa goes down to old Mexico and watches a bull-fight. Afterwards, she goes to a cantina down the street that serves fresh *cajones* delivered straight from the bullfight.

She had been doing this for years, and one evening, she talks to the maître d and says,

"*What happened? The* cajones *have always been large and tender. Tonight they were small and kind of shriveled up.*"

The maître d says,
"*Madam, the bull does not always lose.*"

∞

In the past, why did they name hurricanes only after women?
When they come, they're hot and breezy.
When they leave, they take the house and car.

A woman's husband dies. She wants the memorial service to be perfect.

The mortician calls her and says,
> *I have him all laid out in the casket and want your approval before the ceremony.*

She goes to the mortuary and says,
> *You did a wonderful job. It's just perfect. The only thing is, I think he'd look a lot better in the suit that the gentleman in the next coffin is wearing.*

The mortician instructs,
> *Step outside and give me a few minutes.*

Five minutes later he calls her back in.

She says,
> *That's perfect. How did you do it so fast?*

The mortician replies,
> *I just swapped heads.*

∞

A guy approaches a lady and says,
> *Would you sleep with me if I gave you $500?*

She thinks for a minute and says, *Okay.*

He asks,
> *Would you sleep with me if I gave you a dollar?*

She replies,
> *What kind of woman do you think I am?*

He says,
> *I think we've already established that. We're just haggling over the price.*

This guy picks up a gal at the bar. After their lovemaking, he asks,

"Am I the first man you've ever slept with?"
She answers,

"You might be. Your face looks familiar."

∞

A psychiatrist is in session with a patient. After six months of intensive therapy, he says,

"You're finally cured."
She shouts, *"I'm so happy! Kiss me."*
He exclaims, *"Kiss you? I shouldn't even be lying here on the couch with you."*

∞

A vagina is like the weather: When it's wet, it's time to come in.

∞

What's the difference between a genealogist and a gynecologist?

The genealogist looks up your family tree, and a gynecologist looks up your family bush.

It's a busy day at the bank. Four masked men rush in brandishing guns. One shouts,

"This is a stick-up. Everyone lie down on the floor."

Everyone is face down, except for one gal lying on her back. Her co-worker elbows her and says,

"This is a stick-up, Honey. It's not the office Christmas party."

∞

This older lady goes to her doctor for an exam.

The doctor says,

"There's no doubt about it. Your 're pregnant. Congratulations. I have your husband on the phone, so you can share the good news."

She yells, *"Gimme that phone."*

She screams into the phone:

"You horny old goat. You went and got me pregnant."

A quavering voice on the other end:

This blonde gal is driving her car, and she gets pulled over. She rolls down her window, and the cop is unzipping his pants.

She exclaims, *"Oh no! Not another breathalizer test!"*

∞

Four men are playing golf. They all tee off, and are down at the green putting.

Three women are teeing off, and this one gal whacks the ball really hard and sees it heading straight for one of the men. She yells *"Fore!"* but she's too late. She goes running down and sees the man writhing around on the green, his hands clasped in his crotch.

"I'm so, so sorry, she says. *"I'm a physical therapist. Let me see what I can do to help."*

She reaches down, unzips his fly, and proceeds to give him a slow, sensual massage. A few minutes later she says, *"How's that?"*

He answers, *"That was terrific, but my thumb still hurts like hell."*

A housewife keeps berating her maid. Finally the maid has had enough, and she says,

"According to your husband, not only am I prettier than you are, I'm a better cook and housekeeper."

The wife says, *"Is that so?"*

The maid continues, *"Not only that. I'm a better lover than you are too."*

The wife asks, *"My husband said that?"*

The maid replies, *"No, I got that from the gardener."*

∞

A grandmother is conversing with her granddaughter, and as they talk, she says that she and grandpa still lead an active sex life.

The granddaughter says,

"At your age, I'd stop. It could be fatal."

A week later she's reading the obituaries and finds out her grandfather is deceased. She calls her grandma up to offer her condolences. She says,

"I'm sorry, but I did warn you that this could happen."

The grandma replies, *"Poppycock! We used to make love to the rhythm of the church bells every Sunday morning. And we'd still be doing it if that fire truck hadn't whizzed by."*

An ovary is talking to her sister:
  "Are you fond of music?"

Her sister says, *"Not particularly. Why do you ask?"*

The ovary answers, *"Because two nuts are trying to
  push an organ up here."*

∞

Sister Marilyn has led an exemplary life on earth. She
winds up in heaven playing her harp on a cloud. She
hears a blood-curdling scream and says,
  "Good God, St. Peter! What was that?"

St. Peter replies,
  *"That's nothing. We've had to drill some holes in this
  guy's skull to attach his new halo."*

She is shaken, but goes back to playing her harp. She
hears another scream, louder than the first.
  "Good God, St. Peter! What was that?" she cries.

St. Peter says,
  *"That's nothing. We had to drill some holes in this guy's
  shoulders to attach his new wings."*

The sister exclaims,
  "Forget that. I'm going to hell."

St. Peter tells her,
  *"You know, if you go to hell, you'll get raped and sod-
  omized down there."*

The Sister says,
  "No problem! I already have the holes for that."

Four middle-age mothers are bragging about their sons.

The first mother proudly states,

"My son is a priest and everyone addresses him as 'Father.'"

The second mother says,

"My son is a bishop. They address him as 'Your Grace.'"

The third mother adds,

"My son is a cardinal and they call him 'Your Eminence.'"

The fourth mother brags,

"My son is a Chippendale Hardbody. Women take one look at him and say, 'My God!'"

A guy is racing around the corner in the hallway of a nice hotel. A gal is coming in the opposite direction, and, as they run into each other, he elbows her in the breast. The guy starts apologizing profusely, and she says,

"If your penis is as hard as your elbow, I'm in room 115."

∞

A therapist invites four women and their children for free therapy sessions. He tells the first woman,

"I see you named your daughter Candy. You obviously have issues with food."

The second woman comes in with her daughter, and he says,

"I see you named your daughter Penny. You must have issues with money."

The third woman comes in with her daughter, and he says,

"I see you have issues with drugs. That's why you named your daughter Crystal."

The fourth woman turns to her son and says,
"Come on Dick. Let's get out of here!"

A gal is wearing a tight mini-skirt and she's trying to board the bus. It's so tight she can't raise her leg high enough to get on the first step. She reaches back and unzips the back of her skirt and tries once more to get up on the step, but to no avail. She reaches back and unzips it more, but when she lifts her leg, she still can't reach the step.

The man behind her grabs her by the waist and bodily lifts her to the lowest step. She turns to him, seething in anger, and says,

"How dare you put your hands on my body? I don't even know you."

He says,

"I don't know you either, but after you unzipped my fly twice I kinda' figured we was friends."

∞

A mother and daughter are at the doctor for an exam and the doctor says,

"There's no doubt about it. Your daughter's pregnant."

The mother insists, *"Impossible! She's never even kissed a boy."*

The doctor stands, staring intently out the window.

The mother asks, *"Doctor, what are you looking at?"*

The doctor replies,

"The last time this happened, a star came out in the east and three wisemen appeared. I'm not going to miss it this time."

Men and Women,
Bars, Parties,
Old People,
and
Animals

Sally had just started her monthlies, and she had no idea what was happening. She confided in her best friend, Johnny, and he said,

"Let me take a look."

She pulled down her panties, and he looked around and said,

"I'm not a doctor or anything, but it looks to me like someone ripped your balls off."

∞

This guy goes into the pharmacy to pick up a pack of condoms. He puts it on the register, and the cashier, who is conscientious about her job, asks,

"Are you sure this is the right size?"

The guy says, *"I didn't know they came in different sizes."*

She takes him behind the counter and checks him out, then gets on the intercom and says, *"Package of medium-size condoms on register four."*

The next man in line says he's not sure either, so she checks him out behind the counter and announces on the intercom, *"Package of large condoms on register four."*

A teenager in line is listening to all this and says he's not sure either, so she takes him behind the counter to check him out and, soon after, announces on the intercom,

"Clean-up on aisle four."

A gal went to a bar and saw a gentleman drinking champagne. She says,

"I see you're celebrating. I'm celebrating too. May I join you?"

The man asks, *"What are you celebrating?"*

She replies, *"I've been trying to get pregnant now for years. I just went to a gynecologist who told me I'm pregnant. So what are you celebrating?"*

He says, *"For years I haven't had any baby chicks in my chicken ranch and this spring, all my hens have little chicks trailing behind them."*

She asks, *"To what do you attribute your good fortune?"*

He says, *"I switched cocks."*

She says, *"What a coincidence!"*

Two divorcées meet up at a department store. Mary says,

"I don't know how you do it, Sally, but you have all these men flocking around you, and I haven't been laid since my divorce. What's your secret?"

Sally states,
"Mary, this is the 80s. I see some good-looking man, and I sashay up to him and tell him I have an itchy pussy."

Mary asks, *"Really?"*

Sally says, *"Yeah, by all means."*

A couple days later, Mary is at the supermarket, and there's a good-looking hunk bagging groceries.
"Pardon me, Ma'am," he says. *"Would you like some help out?"*

She says, *"Please."*

He's pushing her basket through the lot, and she sashays up to him and says, *"I've got an itchy pussy."*

He says, *"Pardon me, Ma'am?"*

She repeats louder, *"I've got an itchy pussy."*

He says, *"You'll have to point it out. All those Japanese cars look the same to me."*

A muscle-bound gym rat picks up a gal at a bar and they go back to his house. He pulls off his shirt, flexes his arms, and says,

"See that? That's five tons of dynamite."

He drops his pants and flexes his thighs, and says,

"See that? That's ten tons of dynamite."

He drops his underpants, and she goes running out of the house screaming. He chases her down and says,

"What scared you?"

She replies, "I was afraid to be around all that dynamite with such a short fuse."

∞

A man takes a girl out on a first date to a fancy restaurant with a maître d, a wine steward, and all the trimmings.

A waiter comes to the table to take their order, and she lets out a huge fart and yells at the waiter,

"Stop that immediately!"

The waiter replies suavely,

"Yes madam, which way did it go?"

An old lady calls her vet at 8:00 at night and says,

"The alley cats are out mating on the fence, and they are yowling and making quite a racket. What should I do to make them stop?"

The vet says, *"Tell them they're wanted on the phone."*

The lady asks, *"Do you think that will really work?"*

The vet replies, *"It worked for me."*

∞

The Queen of England was taking a tour of an insane asylum. She noticed all the grounds were absolutely gorgeous and perfectly manicured: the shrubs, the hedges, the flowers. She ran into the head gardener who was also an inmate of the institution and said,

"You're responsible for all these perfectly manicured grounds? With your eye for detail and fine workmanship, I really don't believe you belong here. When I get home, I'm going to research your case and see if I can have you released."

She was just about ready to climb into her limousine, when she got hit in the back of the head with a brick. She turned around to see the gardener standing there with a big grin on his face saying,

*"You won't **forget** me now, will you?"*

Two little people go to Las Vegas, planning to tear up the town: take in a show, go to a bar, pick up a couple of hookers, and take them to their adjoining rooms at the hotel.

The first one is all upset because he can't get it up, and he can hear his buddy next door yelling, "1 2 3 argh. . .

1 2 3 argh…1 2 3 argh. . ."

He thinks, *Darn it, my buddy's having the time of his life next door, and I can't even get it up.*

The next morning, they take the hookers home, and over breakfast his buddy asks,

"*So how did it go last night?*"

He confesses, "*Darn it! I couldn't even get it up.*"

His buddy says, "*You think that's bad? I couldn't even get on the bed.*"

∞

A virginal young man goes to the whorehouse, gets a girl, and they go to the upstairs bedroom. She asks,

"*What will it be: mission, Greek, or 69?*"

He says, "*Let's try 69.*"

They get into position, and she lets out a big fart. They get back in position, and she lets out another one. She looks up, and he's getting dressed.

"*What's the matter?*" she inquires.

He says,

"*I'm sorry, Ma'am. I can't handle 67 more of those.*"

Superman is flying down the east coast to a superheroes convention in Miami. He looks down and sees Wonder Woman lying on a penthouse roof with her legs spread eagle. He swoops down, does her, and continues on to the convention. When he gets there, he tells Batman about his little adventure, and Batman says,

" I bet she was surprised."

Superman replies,

"Not nearly as surprised as Invisible Man was."

∞

Mick Jagger is visiting Hugh Heffner at his Playboy mansion. The door's ajar so he just walks in. He comes into the living room and sees Hugh Heffner getting it on with Dennis Weaver. Mick sings,

"Hey Hey Hugh! Get offa' McCloud!"

The difference between erotic and kinky:
Erotic is when you use a feather; kinky is when you use the whole chicken.

∞

A teenager goes into the pharmacy to get condoms for the first time. The sales clerk shows him the display.

"We have: glow in the dark, sparkly, ribbed, all different colors."

The teen points to one and says,
"I want that one! How much is it?"
The clerk answers, *"$6.95 with tax."*

The teen pales.
"Tacks?? They don't stay on by themselves?"

∞

The most popular guy in a nudist colony is the one who can hold a steaming cup of coffee in each hand *and* a dozen donuts.

∞

The most popular girl is the one who can eat the last donut.

This priest has a parrot with a foul-mouth. He wonders what to do about it. One of his parishioners who also has a parrot suggests,

"My parrot clutches her rosary beads and says prayers all day, so we should introduce them. Maybe mine will be a good influence."

They put the parrots together, and the priest's parrot says,

"Hey Toots, let's get it on."

The other parrot sighs and says,

"Finally! My prayers have been answered."

∞

What's the difference between a porcupine and a Porsche?

The porcupine has the pricks on the outside.

A gal is having a costume party. A guy shows up naked with roller skates on.

The hostess asks,
  "I don't get it. What are you supposed to be?"

The guy says,
  "I'm a pull toy."

∞

A costume party in New York: The hostess wants everyone to dress as an emotion. She's waiting for her guests to arrive. The doorbell rings, and a man is dressed in green: green hat, green shirt, green pants, and green shoes.

The hostess says, *"I see you're green with envy."*

They both laugh, and he walks into the house. The doorbell rings a second time. A gal is decked out in pink.

The hostess says, *"I see you're pink with jealousy."*

The doorbell rings again, and a big man is standing there. He is completely naked with his penis buried in a bowl of custard. She shrugs and says, *"I don't get it."*

The Big Man responds, *"I'm fucking disgusted."*

The doorbell rings a fourth time. A naked man stands there with his penis buried in a hollowed-out pear.

The hostess asks, *"What's **your** story?"*

He says, *"I'm deep in despair."*

On a farm, a horse gets caught in quicksand. He yells to the chicken,

"Bring the farmer's Ferrari, and pull me out of this quicksand."

The chicken tosses him a line, and the Ferrari pulls him out. A week later, the chicken gets mired in the quicksand and yells,

"Horse, go get the farmer's Ferrari and pull me out."

The horse says,

"Nope, no need to. I'll straddle the quicksand."

He straddles the quicksand and lowers his penis, and the chicken grabs onto it and hoists himself up.

And the moral of story:

You don't need a Ferrari to pick up chicks if you're hung like a horse.

∞

A gentleman invited us to a big BBQ. After dinner he passed out marshmallows and, just as we all finished putting marshmallows on our skewers, a fire engine came racing down the street with lights flashing and sirens blaring, and stopped three doors down.

We all raced to the neighbor's house, and witnesed the man and his wife watch all their worldly possessions go up in flames.

They turned around, took one look at the crowd, and began to glare at us. It was then I realized we still had our marshmallow skewers.

A traveling salesman walks into a bar and sees a horse standing there next to a big jar of money that's sitting on the bar. He asks the bartender what's going on. The bartender says,

"We're having a contest to make the horse laugh. It costs ten dollars to enter."

He tosses ten dollars into the jar and whispers in the horse's ear, and the horse breaks into a big horse laugh. The salesman takes his winnings from the jar and leaves.

A couple months later, he's traveling through that part of the country again. The horse is still there at the bar.

The salesman asks,

"You're still having a contest to make the horse laugh?"

The bartender remembers,

"Some fellow was in here a couple months ago and made the horse laugh. Now we're having a contest to make the horse cry."

The salesman tosses ten dollars in the jar and says,

"Do you mind if I take the horse around back?"

They come back in, the horse crying his eyes out. The salesman starts pulling the money out of the jar.

The bartender says,

"I recognize you. You're the one who made the horse laugh. How did you do it?"

The salesman replies,

"Well, the first time I whispered that I was hung longer than he was. Just now I took him around back and showed him."

A white missionary is in deepest, darkest Africa. One morning, two big tribesmen show up at his hut, drag him out, and bring him to their chief.

The missionary asks, *"What's going on here?"*

The chief replies,
"A white baby was born here this morning. You're the only white man within hundreds of miles. Tonight we are going to burn you at the stake."

The missionary responds,
"Just a minute, Chief. See those white sheep grazing on the hillside? All the lambs are white except that little black lamb."

The chief pales, and says, "You no tell. I no tell."

∞

A man came home late, bleary-eyed, after a wild night on the town. He noticed that his wife was already asleep in bed. He crawled in and jumped her bones, went to the bathroom and saw, to his surprise, his wife in the bathtub. He exclaimed,
*"What are **you** doing in **here?**"*
She whispered, *"Be quiet! You'll wake my mother."*
His wife went into the bedroom and asked her mother,
*"Why didn't you **say** anything?"*
Her mother answered,
"I haven't spoken to that man in two years, and I'm not about to start now!"

A peddlar in New York goes door-to-door selling good quality yellow, satin ribbon. He approaches one door, and the man inside agrees to buy a long ribbon to surprise his daughter.

The peddlar says,

"Don't worry, the ribbon will be plenty long. It will reach from the top of my head to the tip of my penis! That's the truth!"

Two weeks later a truck pulls up to the house of the man who bought the ribbon. The peddlar begins to bring in bolts and bolts of ribbon from the truck. The buyer is astounded. He yells,

"I didn't want to buy all that. You tricked me!"

The peddlar says,

"I said the ribbon would reach from the top of my head to the tip of my penis. The truth is, I was born and circumcised in Poland."

Jack and Jill are loyal employees who will always go the extra mile to please their boss. One day he approches Jill and explains, apologetically,

"Work has been slowing down. I won't be able to keep you both. I'm going to have to lay you or Jack off."

She replies,

"You'd better jack off. I have a headache."

A priest and a nun are looking for converts in the Sahara. They rent a camel and head into the desert. They are caught in a blinding sandstorm and, when it subsides, they realize they're hopelessly lost. Then their camel dies.

The priest is thinking, *This is getting really, really grim.* So he raises up his cassock and says,
   "Hey Sister, have you ever seen one of these?"

She says, *"No I haven't Father. What is that?"*

The priest says, *"This is the staff of life."*

The nun responds, *"Well, stick it in that camel and let's get the hell outa' here."*

∞

An Englishman leaving the pub gets propositioned by a streetwalker. They wind up in his car, and a bobby comes along, shines his torch on them, and says,
   "What's going on in there?"

The man replies,
   "Nothing, officer, just shagging the wife."
The bobby says,
   "I'm sorry, I didn't realize it was your wife."

The man responds,
   "Neither did I, until you shined your torch."

How many divers does it take to circumcise a whale?

Four skin divers.

∞

A guy is walking down the beach and a lantern gets washed up. He is rubbing it to get the sand off, and a genie pops out.

The genie says, *"You have one wish."*
The man says,
> *"I've always wanted to travel to Hawaii. The problem is, I'm absolutely terrified of airplanes and I get deathly seasick in boats. My wish is to build a bridge from the mainland so I could go without taking a boat or an airplane."*

The genie responds,
> *"I could do it, but it would take an awful lot of man-power and materials. What would your second wish be?"*

The man says,
> *"I've tried hard all my life, but I've never been able to understand women. My wish would be to **really** understand women."*

The genie replies, *"Do you want that bridge with two lanes or four?"*

Why couldn't the Taliban have sex ed and drivers ed on the same day?

It was too hard on the camels.

∞

A guy is at the supermarket. A gal comes up to him and says,
"I think I have one of your children."

He's thinking and thinking to himself, and finally remembers an incident. He asks her,
"Are you the one on that wild night in the bar when we were getting it on, on the pool table?"

She responds,
"What I meant is that I have your son in my third- grade classroom."

∞

A guy calls up his doctor and says,
"My son has VD and thinks he must have caught it from the maid."

The doctor says,
"Well, don't be too hard on him. Bring him in and I'll fix him up."

The father says,
"Well, I've been fooling around with the maid, myself."
The doctor replies,
"Well, then both of you come in and I'll fix you both up."

The father recalls,
"Actually, I think my wife might have it too."

The doctor exclaims, *"Oh shit! that means we all have it!!!"*

What do you get when you cross human DNA with goat DNA?

You get kicked out of the petting zoo?

∞

Why do lawyers wear neckties?

To keep the foreskin from creeping up over their faces.

∞

BB King's girlfriend is looking for a birthday present for him. It's hard to find, because he already has or could buy anything he wants. She goes to a tattoo artist, and has a big "B" tattooed on her left buttock and a matching "B" on her right.

She takes BB over to her place that night, and wines and dines him. He's already in bed and she says,

"BB, I have a surprise for you."

She slips her panties down and bends over, and BB says,

"Who the fuck is BOB?

∞

Strip poker: the more you lose the more you have to show.

∞

What's the difference between a lawyer and a hooker?

The hooker stops fucking you after you're dead.

There's a hole in the wall in a nudist colony.

Officers are looking into it.

∞

This guy picks up a gal at the bar. They head over to her house and are in bed together. They hear this huge gorilla stomping upstairs to the bedroom.

She exclaims, *"Oh my God! It's my husband!"*

He asks, *"Is there a window or a door up here?"*

She replies, *"No."*

He inquires, *"Where would you like one?"*

∞

What do sex and air have in common?

You don't miss either one until you're not getting any.

∞

A guy walks into a bar, and King Kong is sitting on a barstool. He sits down next to Kong and says,

   "I'm a huge fan. Can I talk to you?"

King Kong replies,

   "Yes, but just for a minute. I have a plane to catch."

A policeman and policewoman are walking their beat and she says,

"Darn, I left my panties at the precinct. We'll have to go back for them."

The policeman responds,

"Not to worry. We have a canine unit. Hike your skirt up and give him a sniff, and he will retrieve them for you."

The dog takes a good sniff and bounds back to the precinct. They wait for five minutes, ten minutes, and fifteen minutes later, they hear a siren. The dog comes into view with something in his mouth and a bunch of squad cars behind him. As he gets closer, they realize it's the desk sergeant's balls.

∞

Why did the worm take judo lessons?

He wanted to learn how to flip the bird.

∞

A young couple is at the drive-in theater. They are necking, petting, getting hot and heavy.

She asks, *"Do you want to get in the back seat?"*

He answers, *"Heck no! I want to stay up here with you!"*

There's a trial for a rape case, and all the jurors are assembled. The judge asks the victim,

"In your words, what did the defendant say to you?"
She replies,

"I can't, your honor. It's way too embarrassing. Can I write it down?"

He says Okay, and she writes it on a paper (The note says: 'I'm going to rip your clothes off and have my way with you.'). The bailiff takes the note to juror number one. It works its way around to the woman who is the eleventh juror, and she sees that the twelfth juror is fast asleep. She elbows him awake and hands him the note.

The judge taps his gavel and says,

"Will juror number twelve please return the note to the bailiff."

Juror number twelve says to the judge,
"I can't, your honor. It's way too personal."

∞

What is the difference between beer nuts and deer nuts?
Beer nuts have gone up to $5.00 a bag,
but deer nuts are still under a buck.

∞

My neighbors aren't aware of it yet, but they're going to be starring in a porn movie on the internet.

An older couple is celebrating their fortieth wedding anniversary. They're at the same hotel where they had their first encounter. After breakfast the wife says,

"Let's go into the back alley and make love against that fence like we did forty years ago."

They're going at it, and this kid walking down the alley says,

"What stamina. What endurance. I don't know how you old folks do it."

The man responds, *"Forty years ago that fence wasn't electrified."*

∞

The chief medical officer is walking down the corridor of a hospital, when a nun bolts out of an exam room and runs screaming down the corridor.

He walks into the room, and says to the doctor giving the exam, *"What's going on here? "*

The doctor replies, *"Well, I just told the nun she was pregnant."*

The chief asks, *"So is the nun pregnant?"*

The doctor responds, "No, but it sure cured her hiccups."

A priest was invited to preach a sermon in a church in New York City. They pick him up at the airport in a limo, check him into a five-star hotel, and drive him to St. Paul's Cathedral to deliver a sermon.

Afterwards, they take him back to his room. He walks in, and there's a woman in his bed wearing nothing but a smile. He gets on the phone to the manager and says,

"This is an outrage. I'm a distinguished priest. I'm going to get to the bottom of this, and heads are going to roll when I do!"

He looks over, and the lady is out of bed getting dressed.

He says,

"Where are you going, Miss? Nobody was talking to you."

∞

There was a young man named Blair,

who was doing his gal on the stair.

On the 21st stroke,

the bannister broke,

and he finished her off in mid-air.

A scientist in New York City was concocting a serum to make porpoises immortal. The main ingredient had to be harvested from baby seagulls as soon as they hatched. He had to go to Florida to get the newborn gulls, so he could rush them back to his lab in New York and extract the necessary ingredient.

He completed his mission, and while driving through a state game reserve, he saw a lion lying in the middle of the road. He stopped, honked his horn repeatedly, then got impatient, and ran over the lion. The ranger saw him do it, and arrested him. And do you know what they charged him with?

Taking young gulls across the state lion
for immortal porpoises.

∞

There was a young man named Kent,
whose dick was so long that it bent.
To save all the trouble,
he shoved it in double,
and instead of coming, he went.

A really burly construction worker is wearing a dainty diamond stud in his ear. The foreman comes up and says,

"That looks absolutely ridiculous on you. How long have you been wearing that stud?"

He says, *"Ever since my wife found it in our bed."*

∞

A gay guy is sashaying down the sidewalk in front of a construction site. This brawny redneck construction worker hollers out,

"Hey faggot! Where are your pearls?"

He shouts back, *"Pearls with corduroy? Are you mad?"*

∞

Why are men like floors?
You lay them right the first time,
and you can walk all over them
for the rest of your life!

A guy buys a motorcycle, and the seller gives him a tube of vaseline and tells him,

"If it rains, be sure to put vaseline on the chrome so it won't rust."

He is invited for dinner at the home of his girlfriend's parents. When he gets there he sees dirty dishes every-where— piled high in the sink, countertops, and the floor. He asks his girlfriend,
"What's with all the dishes?"

She says,
"Don't say a word. My folks are fighting, and the first person to talk has to do the dishes."

They sit down to eat. Everyone is dead silent. He thinks to himself: *What an opportunity! I'll just do my girlfriend on the table.*

He does and, sure enough, no one says a word. He thinks, *M m m...Her mom's lookin' awful good.*

So he does the mom on the table too, and no one says a word. The father and the girlfriend are looking very upset.

Just then, he looks outside and sees that it's starting to rain. He pulls the vaseline out of his pocket, and the father gets a horrified look on his face and says,

"I'll do the fucking dishes."

Four young bikers, all covered with tattoos and clad in leather, were sitting at their favorite table at the pub, quaffing their pints. This old man walked in, sat down, and addressed the brawniest one,

"I saw your mum last night. She was lookin' hot."

The biker was seething and gritting his teeth, and his friends thought he was about to deck the old man.

The old man continued, *"I'm going back to see your mum tonight, and we're going to have a wild time."*

The next day the bikers were at the pub again, and the old man walked in and said,

"I did your mum for hours last night, and it was a wild time."

The brawny biker got really upset and said,

"Go home, Dad. You're drunk!"

∞

There was a young harlot named Sue
who filled her vagina with glue.
Said she, with a grin,
"If they'll pay to get in,
then they'll pay to get out of it too."

I always wanted to be the last man on earth,

just to see if all those women were telling the truth.

∞

A mafia boss had an accountant who was deaf and dumb. Everything was doing fine until he decided to have another accountant check the books. He found out that the deaf and dumb one had ripped him off for a couple million dollars.

He told a couple of his goons to bring the accountant and his brother (who did sign language) to his house.

The mafioso addressed the accountant (the brother translating everything in sign language),

"I know you stole two million dollars, and I want it back!"

The accountant said, *"You must be mistaken. I never stole anything."*

The mafioso pulled out a pistol and held it up to the accoutant's head, and said,

"Listen here, punk. I'm gonna blow your brains out. Before I do, my goons are gonna work you over real good."

The accountant started shaking and sweating profusely, and signed to his brother, saying,

"The money's in a satchel in my closet."

The brother told the mafioso,

"My brother says you ain't got the balls."

A plane is on its way to Toronto when a blonde in economy stands, moves up the aisle to first class, and sits down. The flight attendant is watching this, and asks to see her ticket.

The flight attendant says,

"You have paid for economy and you'll have to move back there."

The blonde responds,

"I'm blond, I'm beautiful, I'm going to Toronto, and I'm staying right here."

The flight attendant goes to the cockpit, and tells the pilot and co-pilot there's a blonde bimbo sitting in first class who refuses to move back to economy. The co-pilot goes to her and explains the situation, but the blonde repeats,

"I'm blonde, I'm beautiful, I'm going to Toronto, and I'm staying right here."

The co-pilot returns to the cockpit, and tells the pilot they should probably alert the police so they can arrest her on arrival, for not listening to reason.

The pilot asks,

"You say she's blonde? I'll handle this. I speak blonde. I'm married to one."

He goes back to the lady, whispers something to her, and she says, *"Oh, I'm sorry,"* and quickly moves back to her seat in economy.

The flight attendant and co-pilot are amazed, and ask him, "What did you tell her?"

The pilot says, *"I told her first class isn't going to Toronto!"*

Eve sat anxiously in the Garden of Eden waiting for Adam.

Finally, late in the night he returned to his vexed and agitated mate.

Eve asked, *"Where have you been? Is it another woman?"*

Adam reasoned: *"But Eve, you are the only woman in the Garden…nay, in the whole world."*

"Come closer," she implored. *"Let me count your ribs!"*

The End
(or the beginning)

Acknowledgements

I owe a debt of gratitude to Laurie C who edited, drew the illustrations, and produced the book.

She built a fire under me when I was slacking. She said: *"We're not getting any younger, you know. Let's get on with this!"*

I'm grateful to my wife, Denise, who proofread and corrected the text, cover to cover.

Laurie and Denise helped me realize a childhood dream. This book would not have happened without them. I love them both.

Would you like to see your joke in print?

Email it to: klymerkit@yahoo.com. If I use your joke in my next edition, I will pay you $20.00.

Best of Luck,
Kittrick

Made in the USA
Columbia, SC
20 May 2024

35545985R00065